roots
and
tendrils

Heidi Dellaire

ISBN 978-1-54395-760-0 eBook 978-1-54395-761-7

To those who brave the inner workings of the heart.

Contents

Willow

"false love or love forsaken"

Abandoned

I can't pinpoint the exact moment I abandoned myself.

It was after my failed relationship. As I reflect back, I think that's about when it started. I signed up for a course in the Universal Lessons of Abandonment without the awareness I was even enrolled, and already paying dues.

My guilt and shame surrounding my failed relationship became part of my identity. My guilt for having blown up my life, and for hurting another, stuck to me like dog shit in the crevasses of my shoe.

In the last decade, there have been a myriad of lovers that have come into my life. All seemed like viable candidates for partnership... each one ready to love me for me. Each one ready to explore the depths of my heart and open the door for me to welcome them in.

I lied to myself about them all.

Each one of them ended up leaving a mark, a scar or a lesson, right down to the last narcissistic asshole. I attracted the emotionally unavailable, the self-obsessed egoist, the ghoster, the gas-lighter, and the "my trauma trumps anything else on the planet" lover. Some came to me, not just once, a few of these themes were revisited.

There seems to be an assignment that I took on with each of them. Each one getting me closer to a passing grade. Each one ripping my heart apart. Each one hurting me and pushing me closer to myself, closer to the truth.

I had abandoned myself.

I looked for love outside of myself. I searched for love everywhere but where I needed to find it the most. They came as an assignment: look in the mirror.

Looking in the mirror now, I know I have been here all along. I just needed to open my own heart to see, to see myself.

Welcome home.

Welcome to love.

There comes a moment in time when
You realize no person, place, doctrine or guru
Is going to save you.
Only you can save you.
Be your own guru.

Caged

Your last spoken words still fill my ears,
Reverberating as a sharp echo from the distance.

I am a piranha.
I am a predator.
I am a shark.
I am an emotional vampire.
I see the bodies of the people I have destroyed and
I want to wash them away so
I don't have to look at the pile anymore.

I have become just that to you,
A body on the pile washed away to ease your pain.

Piranha, predator, shark

I wonder what you will tell your next lover.

Piranha, predator, shark
Shark
Shark

I know what I will tell mine:
She spat fear like venom,
From deep behind the bars of her self-imposed prison.
Without knowing how to love herself, it came out sideways.

I loved her. I could feel the softness behind the wild.

Fire Ants

As I watch and listen, the blood leaves my hands
no feeling in them...cold...numb.
My body is on fire, yet I can feel the blood start to leave.
I witness an eye exchange...recoil. I rub my hands trying to warm them,
for I fear the fire ants.
Nothing works, they are on their way. I struggle to stay seated and
I see other hands that aren't mine.
The scene changes. I watch. The sounds leave and I am in the bubble. No
one can hear me, no one can hear them as they march. From inside my
chest, they pierce through my veins and get sucked into the chambers of
my heart. From atria to ventricle they are pushed through.
I can't stop it now. They are on their way.
I look again. Locked. Frozen. Bubble. Beautiful.
I am screaming on the inside but no one else hears. Slowly they make
their way and the burning starts. They march and open the capillaries of
my fingers. My hands are now on fire. They are screaming to be heard.
I want to lay them on you. Can't you feel the heat from these hands.
Locked. Don't go. Don't do it. Stay. The burn is unbearable. It hurts.
The fire ants have you in their sights.

Lessons

It's hard for me to let go of people,
Even ones who are toxic to me.

There's a weird shame in cutting someone out of my life.
Aren't we supposed to love everyone?
Isn't that my job?
I am a fixer after all.

It's hard for me to let go of people,
Even ones who are toxic to me.

They stick a little harder than most.
They get to me.
They get to me in my core.
They bring out the parts of me I dislike.

It's hard for me to let go of people,
Even ones who are toxic to me.

There is something in them that I love.
There is something in them that I hate.
They reflect the parts of me I still need to work on.
I can't do this with them in my life.

Now, it's becoming less hard for me to let go of people.
I am learning to let go of the toxic ones,
and I am loving myself in the process.

Layers

The loud boom of metal trap doors clanging open startles me,
As I feel myself release to you.
I have been walking alone in a depth of quiet
Yet here you are enveloped in the same quiet
Here we lie silenced by our gaze
Layer by layer, in our vulnerable nakedness, we reveal all to the other.
I try to catalog all that you show me in this deep gaze.
I won't remember it all.
I want to see it again,
Will I get a second reveal?

Fading Into Morning

Midnight passes
Minutes into hours tick away at my heart -
Faster and faster they go

My hands touch you as they always do
But tonight, all is voltaic
The moon softly pours in on top of us...I feel your pull

Lips and skin afire
Electric arcs of light between us
I can't get enough of you
I can't breathe you in fast enough
My heart stays with you tonight.

Wakefulness overcomes me
The moon descends
I watch it fall from the sky

Light begins to take her place
My soul becomes weary
For I dread what comes next

"I love you", I hear
And my heart snaps like a brittle twig
It's not enough in the last electric hours before morning
My spirit fades with the diminishing light of the moon.

Lens

We are caught up in the story we tell ourselves
We can't see beyond our own anecdote.
We set rigid parameters around the lens we look through-
Spouting off about someone else
To everyone else
Making up a story
Only seen through our self-limiting beliefs-
A narrow lens.
Check yourself.
Check your story.
The beauty of storytelling- you can change the narrative.
Open the lens and look with love instead of fear.
Fear tends to talk too much.

When you ask the universe for signs,
Don't ignore them when they show up.

Spoons

We created this game before we met.
Who would be the inside spoon, who would be the outside spoon?
It was a game of longing, a way to be close
Shortening the distance across the airwaves.
Each night we would end our call with the question,
Inside spoon or outside spoon?

You would choose inside spoon every time, even after we actually met.
I acquiesced, and you never knew
How much I wanted to be the inside spoon.
How much I wanted to be held by you.

Later I would realize you are not a spoon at all.
You are a knife.
Double-edged like a razor and ready to slice
Anyone who got too close to your heart.
There was no getting close to you from either the inside or the outside
Without feeling the presence of the blade in wait.

This is how the game has ended.

Clean

The humid air wraps around me with its denseness as I walk down
the front steps.
My bare feet touch the warm pavement and I look up into the night sky.
The encroaching full moon looms overhead.
As I stare at her luminescence,
drops from heaven begin to dampen my face.
The drops are warm and loving,
The type of rain that invites you to bathe in her arms.
The type of rain that begs you to let it all go.
The type of rain that, as it drips down your face from your wet hair says,

"Don't worry. Everything will be okay.
Let me wash you clean from it all.
You don't have to do anything but stand here.
I will shower you in the teardrops of the universe.
I will shower you with the love of the world.
I will wash away all the ugliness placed upon your soft heart."

I point my face to the sky and let the rain wash me clean.

Wormwood
"absence, bitter-sorrow"

Near Light

The light became a gift
A print, an imprint, a beautiful scene
I've given it two names;
The Shattering and
Let the Light In

Depending on who looks
Who feels
And who lets go
It can take on either of the two

With the shattering, comes the letting of light
The cracking open from the deep well
To be shattered…shattered like tempered glass

We all bask in the want to share our freedom
Freedom to be seen
Freedom to be heard
Freedom to be understood
We want to share that freedom with another soul
Do you dare enough to be this brave?

I write this for me
I write this for you
I write this for everyone
For we all go through a shattering
A cracking open
A letting in of light,
Which becomes a gift
A print, an imprint, a beautiful scene

Hope

As the sun peaks over the tops,
The trees form a crystalline palace of light
Glistening, beaming, shimmering light
There it sits on the horizon –Hope

We've been told we shouldn't have it
Hope seems elusive at times
Yet we hang onto it
Grasping at hope for want of a better tomorrow

Stickiness hides behind Hope
A longing for something that may not come
And with Hope comes Fear
Fear that things may get worse, fear of getting hurt.

Is that true?
What do I believe?
What do you believe?
What lies behind or beyond Hope?

Hope turns to Optimism as I let Fear go
Stitch sadness to the wind and let it fly

Crepuscular rays of light announce the gloaming
A new year's moon is on the rise
My intentions are set
I meet you where you are with an open heart

**You can't expect the mind
to do the
heart's work.**

Prelude to Midwinter

The silence of this room overwhelms me
A vacuum of time
Hearing only the resonant sound of my blood moving
Beat by beat through my body
Air pushing through my lungs
My senses awaken, for I can see in this darkness
Light
Brilliant shades of indigo and violet ebb between us
Your back faces me
Trusting
Feeling the heat surge from within me
My hands seek you out
Searching for that place that hums
And here, in this prelude to midwinter, I am caught
Time slows
Flesh and bone dissolve
Leaving only the essence of you
The flame in my core escapes through my hands
Drawn like a magnet
With gentle hands ablaze
My light connects with yours
This room now fills with sound
Air releasing from your being
I inhale the encapsulating light
Sleep can come now
For the night is no longer dark
Peace instills, while waiting for day to break.

Power Outage

As the power flickers and finally fades, I have time to just sit in the dark.
It seems as though I have been sitting in the dark for a while now-
hiding, falling in and out, regrouping, waiting,
and trying to control my surroundings.
With a power outage and a blaring car alarm to shock my senses,
I am left to agree.
There are things that one can't control.
Yes, I can influence them with the choices I make, but I can't control fate.

So, what happens next?

Do I continue to hide, fall in or out, regroup, or wait?
If the choice were truly mine, I would come out of hiding, fall deeply in,
settle, and finally...finally live freely.

Night Vision

for David

Every Wednesday I join your Special Ops Team.
You hand me a pair of night vision goggles.
I whisper, "Rest easy. I'll take watch".

I don my eyewear to survey the scene.
You clutch the wall naked and afraid.
I wrap you tightly in a blanket of love
and whisper again,
"Rest easy. I'll take watch".

For the next 5400 seconds, I pour love into the battlefield.
I touch the tip of the sniper's silencer and bless the one who pulls the
trigger and the one who will receive the hit.
I descend from the nights sky with the paratroopers
to ensure soft landing.
I keep a watchful eye on the serpent approaching Michael's sword.
I ignite his shield in a blaze of red to protect the fallen.

I see you stir as you hear the repetitive hum of the
Black Hawk on approach.
I remind you as you turn from the wall, "Rest easy. I'll take watch".

Every Wednesday, I soften the battlefield.
Every Wednesday, I don my night vision.
Every Wednesday, I carry the load on my back for 5400 seconds.
Every Wednesday, I join your Special Ops Team.
Every Wednesday, I become the Watchman.

Window

A window in its crudest form is an opening in a door or wall that allows the passage of light & if not sealed the passage of air and sound.

One look at the window to the mountain and I am transported to my spirit self. I'm taking flight on the wings of a hawk catching speed as I hurl towards the window to your soul.

Wind tunnels create a deafening sound as I gain speed towards the entrance. And as I enter, all goes quiet and I am greeted by a mountain shrouded in cloud. A circling of geese protects the view to the snow-covered crag. They represent the journey of the great quest. Your spirit form dwells behind these wispy clouds creating order in chaos. I envision you atop this mountain in seated meditation…waiting.

Hazy shimmers of light are cast through the clouds as my winged form approaches. The screeching cry of my hawk asks for entrance. All becomes clear. Dreams and visions flash before me. Movement, sound, light, emotion. Your stories move so fast before my bird's eye that nothing and everything stays all at once.

A voice calls me back. I don't want to go. I just got here. I have just started to see. It's calling me back to standing form. Just as I see you looking up from your mountain nook, I am rushed back through your window, your portal of light, air and sound.

I hear myself ask, "Did you take all of these photos?" Already knowing what the answer will be. I am brought back to the order of now with my feet in the present and my wings in spirit. I turn to you as we continue to make breakfast. You tell me stories of other photos. Your body brushes against me and I wonder if these two worlds would be allowed to collide…spirit and form. I have felt your form. The colorful reel of your spirit self still plays on the wings of this flying bird with an eye cast toward the window of your soul.

Unfurl

I watch you open to the sun-
then retreat into a ball
at first sight of your shadow.

When you fan your leaves, you reach for the sun
and all the light that it brings,
Nourishing every part of your being.

But when the dark thoughts come,
you retreat back to the ball.
Wrapping your leaves around yourself.

I see you ripping parts of
yourself off-
Just to try to find yourself.

Your darkness is hard to hold.
Your darkness is hard to hold up.
It's too heavy for me.

Curled up in a ball
The sun cannot shine enough light
To coax you to unfurl
Into the beauty that lies beneath.

Flickering Light

Our eyes lock and people notice. We can't help it...I know I can't.
You pulled your hair back. That makes me smile.
I am loud and silly.
I watch you.
The lights dim and you are cast in shadow
with the dance of flickering candle light.
I watch your hands and how they hold your wine glass.
I feel them move across my skin.
I watch your body language and your head roll down as she tells the story
(you can't save her) and then sings "Soul Lover".
I watch you with your back turned.
I see the light as it bounces off the side of your face.
I watch you and gaze at the woman I want to kiss so desperately. I want
to feel your skin against mine. I want to feel your hands on me...in me...
pulling me forever closer.
The waiter catches me in my bubble- entangled in a daydream.
I cried at the table tonight.
My bomb shelter is being sprayed by metal shrapnel
from the exploding box in my chest.
I want you close.
I want to hold you tightly to me, but sometimes, it isn't enough.
It isn't enough.
I want all of you

Roots and Tendrils

Your love pierced through the soil of my heart
Each word, each look, grew quickly
The shoots, the roots, the tendrils
Pushed through and held tight

A feeling of connectedness for the first time
But the weight of water drew you away
The final word you uttered was love
Leaving the haunting grasp of the tendrils of your heart

I don't know where to look
My words just melt into the earth
You were the last
To take up root

You have to heal your own heart
and then the right things
will come into your life.

The Observer

There is a heart that holds all of the answers I am seeking.
Not just some commonplace heart,
but my own.
I used to plunge into the depths of other hearts
seeking knowledge and love.
Watching, listening, cataloguing other people's pain and joy.
I took it all on as my own,
while searching for a love of my own.

I lived inside a world where all I saw and felt was the outside world.
The outside world became mine.
I lived in a world where I felt too much.
I felt it all, a bleeding empath
unable to distinguish my own feelings from those of others.
I was the observer of every life and
feeler of every emotion including my own.
To seek happiness and love from everything outside of me,
It was all that I knew.

That way of living has passed.
My heart found too much heartbreak with that kind of living.
My new life finds me diving headfirst and deeper into my own heart.
Into the unexplained chambers.
Into the depths of my divine, authentic and messy self.
Seeking my own truth and knowledge.
Freedom comes with this way of living.

Squirrel

Today, I watched the squirrels in my yard.
I watched one in particular.
He chased his squirrel friends.
He was chased in return.
He was busy.
He had trees to climb, new leaf buds to eat, food storage to keep up and
tree hopping to perform.
Never once was he worried about being loveable or being enough for
his mates.
He was just busy being a squirrel.
Today, I want to be a squirrel.

Heartbreak

Dear universe and all things heavenly, I request a cease and desist on the heartbreak. While I know this is an impossible request, I ask anyway.

We often don't talk about our heartbreak because we are afraid of letting someone see behind our masks, afraid to let someone see our shadows, afraid to dive deep and be open and vulnerable. Afraid to let someone witness us in our most raw and authentic form while exposing our tender hearts. We are afraid of being hurt.

Today, I am opening up. I am opening up to all who are feeling heartbreak at this time.

I know many of you.

I have been on a journey of loving wide open…loving in a way that exposes my heart and keeps me vulnerable to all I must experience… loving wide open and being witness to others heartbreak and joy.

The journey has culminated as a test into the realm of heartbreak. I've had the pleasure of being given many gifts of love. Unexpected.

Some stayed; others were rapidly hauled out of my hands. Unexpected.

Now I find myself in this place of sheer grief and loss. Unexpected.

It's a struggle to feel defeat, and I just sit in this place. It's a fuzzy place, one I don't understand. Why am I here now?

Then dear universe, you took my dog. There are no words. Low blow.

Unexpected.

I sit here in this vast, quiet space feeling tired. My heart is weary.

I sit here feeling a little lost, not knowing what I need and all I can say is, "I surrender". I surrender to whatever you bring on the day, whether it is joy, sadness, laughter, amazement, wonder, challenge, gentleness, synchronicity, creativity or just this extreme quiet.

I don't know what to do. That may be the point…
to sit and to be witness to myself.
To sit and love my own heartbreak and loss, while witnessing our universal heartbreak and joy.

I am grateful to feel it all.

Love wide open.

Heart Cleanse

When I throw my heart into the ocean, I always feel clean.

Clean in a way that only a hard bashing and scraping
against the rocks can provide.
They don't just clean you,
they rip off things that couldn't possibly hold on.

You're left with nothing but a raw place. Just raw.
Raw in a way that will take several scabs to heal over.
Continuous peeling and healing
of a wound that is deep.
A wound that still plagues you.
A wound that is so deep you don't know if it will ever truly heal.
It may just slough a scab for the rest of your life
never fully forming a scar.

Some wounds never quite heal and you are
forced to carry them around with you.
They lay dormant
and sometimes they bleed.
The wound clings close, like a child, struggling to find wings

A part will always remain
Unhealed.

Floating

Time moves quickly when you aren't paying attention.
The spring thaw brings eiders to the ocean's edge to
play in the waves, swimming in pairs.

A female perches on a rock to preen herself,
as the tide makes its gradual advance.

She waits until her feet can no longer hold on-
the waves lift her,
she looks outward
and floats away

Adrift without a mate.

Owl Speak

If I correspond at midnight, I will most likely wake you.
As I lie here, I want to fall into the wonder of words and imagination.
What pearl gets shared with the outside world?
Will anyone understand my love of light and dark
Or the texture of sinew, flesh and spirit?

Who understands the distance, in footsteps,
to get to the bare maple tree ahead?
Who questions the depth of what I feel when I look up to the sky?
Who?

After months of wondering, I received the answer.
I have known all along.

There is no magical who.
There is only the wonder deep within.
I am the who I have been searching for.

Moonflower
"dreaming of love"

Life

Today I watched a dragonfly rest its wings on the dock.
Looking through its transparent wings, I realized how precious life is.
Its lifespan, so short, yet so full of vigor and vitality.

People often do nothing with their lives for years, or if ever.
If we were fully alive like a dragonfly, we would live differently.
We would live each second carefree and as if it were our last.

Flitting about this way and that.
Moving quickly and then coming to a standstill
while we idle for a mere moment.
Zipping off quickly in a new direction chasing after our dreams
with sheer delight.

We would move with no true hesitation or stop.
Just a pause before moving forward without fear of our demise.
Excitement for what lies in our path at each turn.
Excitement for the journey ahead.

Linger

How do you measure the time of a touch, a hug, or a stare?
What is too long? Does time reveal the thoughts inside my head?
Sideways glances and a peaceful understanding of who looks back at me.
I have shared so many conversations with you that have never been
spoken aloud or heard.
Who is your favorite author? Have you read Mary Oliver's poetry? Can
you feel the energy that flows between us when we touch? Can I tell you
more about the moon, the mountains and the silence? Do you feel me as I
sit behind you? What would happen if I touched the nape of your neck?
The bass line pounds in my ear.
Do you know that I crave conversation with you? People watching,
observing, and cataloging. Words. Cerebral stimulation, please!
I remember and now deliberately hold you longer. I want to linger here.
Beware that fire you speak of.
It attracts, takes hold and eventually burns you down.
True Match? Flash point.
Scales out of balance. I crave love as you do...necessary for my survival.
Droplets speckle the floor.
Tame?
Never.

I want to meet someone brave enough to love me;
brave enough to let down their walls
and hold space for us both to flourish.

Radiant

It is only after leaving that I realize completely your presence.
With a sudden smile and shared interest,
your radiance emits a searing heat,
a brilliant green and glittering orange heat.
This radiant heat comes in vibrant color and waves.
Fire behaving as water.
Water behaving as fire.

It is lustrous, dazzling and deeply penetrating.
I hear my words outside of this realm, for I have lost my voice for a
moment. A loss of words caught up on a fiery light that encompasses
your being.

You smile again and take me to {Bali, Italy, Scotland}
anywhere your colored dreams want to go. Where will you take me?
What do you want me to see? A glimpse has been given and I seek more.
I seek all that is light, all that glows. What is ablaze inside of you?
What burns?
What from your resplendent radiance will I see again or be asked
to explore?
Will you ask the same of me?

Cave of Fear

It takes courage to come face-to-face with your soul.
Be brave.

There will be things along the way that you will have to encounter alone,
but you won't actually be alone.

Others before you have walked this path on the quest for freedom.

Along the way, you may doubt yourself.
You may think you have gone crazy.

You won't know who you are anymore, but don't worry.
You will find yourself.
You will heal.
You will learn things about yourself and why you tell yourself
the things you do.
You will become someone new, someone who steps outside of the pain
in search of the truth.
A truth bigger than what we make up in our heads.
A truth bigger than our false beliefs.

Everything will be okay.
You will find the people that belong to you.
You will find your heart again.
You will find your purpose when you come out the other side.
You will step out of the cave of fear into the bright light.
You will step out into freedom.

It takes courage to come face-to-face with your soul.
Be brave.

Her Alchemical Heart

She has no idea the beauty of the silver that shines like flowing rivers throughout her heart.

The shrapnel melted over the years to create lines and beautiful highways of road art.

These are not scars or wounds anymore.

They have woven their way to become transformed into reinforcement and expansion; rivers and oceans of silver in her red pounding heart.

Alchemy has taken over and mixed the two elements together.

Blood and silver combine to form a radiant, glowing orange flame that flickers and flits with speckles of green fanning it from below.

An alchemical blend of darkness and light.

Love lives here in her expanding heart, growing with each silvery shard.

Islands in the Mist

Out there, somewhere, within the shrouding mist, rests an island
An island we all seek out
The one, the only
The one that holds all of the answers within its rocks and
held tight by the sea
Yet we are the ones that hold the answers to the beckoning questions
Deep within our souls, we house many islands in the mist.

As I sit here on this rock with you, I look out and do not worry
what the day will bring
I cannot see the islands, not even with my bird's eye
The mystery of what lays ahead is presented and you invite me to step
through your framework, through the gold leafed frame
of your childhood and love of this land and water
I am guided through the framing by your words,
creating snapshots that fit each frame
There are islands in the mist, moss on the trees, waves lapping the shore
and a breathtaking vista that is within reach.

The only thing that matters is the sharing
The sharing of the human experience
The sharing of what we hold dear
Asking of curious questions
Revealing without fear

My heart is happy that the physical islands were hidden
in the dense cover today
For the journey through your aesthetically pleasing framework allowed us
to create our own island
It's a beauty worth hanging on the wall
Clear of the mist and with 1000 strands to grab onto

Muted

A soft light casts its way into the room
I wake in a strange land, yet all feels familiar
There is a faint sound of a trickling brook that echoes into the room and
gives way to the rise and fall of breath. A breath that is not mine, yet just
as rhythmic
As I turn my head and gaze slowly to the left, a form comes into view in
the shadows of the bed
This form, this spirit, this woman is not just beside me, but touching me.
Our hands are intertwined and as consciousness overtakes me,
I realize that we have been lying this way for hours.
Legs wrapped, hands intertwined and breath rising and falling in unison.
Sleep is elusive as dawn breaks. Black, white and grey shift to color with
the rising fire in the sky.
I can see the vapors of heat rise in the room, your aura sitting just atop
your creamy skin.
If you open your eyes, they will cast a light onto my watchful gaze.
You murmur and turn in closer to me.
My entire left side against your right.
My emotional heart space all aflutter.
I stop my ruminating, take a deeper breath, and drift off as the sun beams
illuminate your bed.
As I drift peacefully into a dream, my vibrations are humming.
I know that soon enough you will stir, awaken me, our lips will meet and
we will say Good Morning.
For that, I am already grateful.

Nothing Matters More Than Love

Is there anything that matters more than love? I believe we often pretend that there are things or ideas that matter more than love. We are given gifts from the universe to rip down the veil of these false ideals. Love will do anything to find you and reach into the depths of your being until you can feel and see that nothing else truly matters. There is nothing that matters more than love.

As you rise on this new day, your neural pathways tingle with an awakening. You search for a label to attach to the energy waves and information that pulses through your body. While these waves wash through you, you attempt to look at them through a conceptual lens. This lens does not focus the way you want it to, for what you really seek is a portal through which you can experience the aliveness that is waking within you, a portal that leads you to the doorway of your heart. For once that door has opened, there is no turning back.

If you walk through that door, you can no longer attach to the feelings of sadness, grief, anger or heartbreak. For what are they really? They are mere representations of fear. Nothing exists in our minds except fear and love. When the door to love has fully opened, fear steps aside. Fear can no longer survive in this environment. The air and darkness that fear thrives upon are stripped away and it vanishes deep into the shadows of who we once were.

Love delivers you an invitation of the grandest kind. Love shows you what you can become as it moves through all of your senses, all of your stored memories, every cell in your being and all that you uniquely encompass. This place that love shows you is sacred and wild within you. It is wild with untamed lands yet to be discovered. It is the light that pierces the darkness of your shadows.

A creative stirring now ripples through you. It ripples and creates waves on the ground that you once held your feet firm upon. You try to label this stirring. What you try to label has never appeared before. It is the divine intelligence of the universe hurtling out of the cosmos to stir the stardust of your soul, requesting your presence within the collective consciousness of the universe.

Step back from the story and bask in the awakening of your inner sacredness. Don't try to name this evolution of your inner being. Take hold of the vulnerability that is presented before you; the vulnerability to accept and love the being that you are without any masks, layers or cover-ups. Remember, you only ever long for your own presence in this world, not for something that appears outside of yourself. There is nothing that matters more than the love of your unique self in the vastness of our universe. There is nothing that matters more than love.

Trust and love are hard to come by in
any relationship
until you learn to
trust and love yourself.

Solstice

Waves of familiarity rush through me.
What does it mean?
What does any of it mean?
I am not supposed to know…until I do.

The day was filled with thoughts that were deep and consuming,
Often, not my own.
A stream of consciousness flowing as the tap, tap, tap of ice fingers
touched my window.

Tap, Tap, Tap.
Tap, Tap, Tap.
Why are you so willing to expose yourself?
Why am I?
Perhaps, we understand this journey to finally be accepted in our
naked form?

Did my honesty disarm you?
Or did it just allow you to unlock all on your own?
Wide Open.
It's the only way to move forward from this self-imposed smothering.

As my head falls into the cradle of soft down,
A chime echoes amongst the tapping.
I read the words delivered as an invitation to explore.

I see and recognize myself in you.
It's familiar and settling
For the first time,
I will sleep all of the hours-
A Sound Solstice Sleep.

Love Letter

Although you might not know it, I tell you "I love you" almost every day, many times a day. It's like poetry that pounds in my heart to be heard. I tell you with the flowing of my blood, the vastness of the universe and the simplicity of my breath. My breath, my air, and my voice rejoice in you when I tell you "I love you".

I remember the first time I felt you near. The ground literally moved, I shifted on my feet as you emerged from shadows into the light. I knew then, my life would be changed forever.

When I tell you "I love you," what I mean is, I want you, forever. The electro-chemical burn of "us" is undeniable. I love the way you feel, taste, smell and breathe. I love the way your silhouette attracts the moonlight in the dark. I love how you hold yourself, still somewhat shy behind that outer Kevlar shell.

When I tell you "I love you", I want you to hear that I want to share a life with you- whatever that may look like. I want us to lift each other toward our goals. I want to feel the electric part of your kiss on my soul. I want to fall asleep with you the way that otters do; holding hands so we won't drift apart.

When I tell you "I love you", I want you to hear how much I respect you. I respect you for everything you have come through. I respect your drive and your passion for the things and ideals you believe in.

When I tell you "I love you", I mean that I love who you are. I love your courage to become who you want to be even though you are fearful. I love the broken cracks of you. I love the whole of you. I want you to know that I will stay as long as it takes for you to trust me. I want to hold you tight when your fears arrive and reassure you that everything will be ok.

When I tell you "I love you", I want you to hear that you are free to be you. I love who you are, as you are. I don't want to change you. If you decide to change, that is your journey and I will be here to adapt to those changes.

There's a place that has been carved out in my heart for you. So, when you are ready to show up in my life, there's a place for you here in my heart.

If I write it here, maybe you will feel it in its most raw form. From my core pours my love and my heart. Do you hear my love beating on the drums? I want to run through the fields to the sound of the pounding. I want you to know this beating inside my chest.

I know I will recognize you when I see you, even though we haven't met before. We will recognize each other, for you just finished writing the same letter.

A Plea for Holding Heart Space

Many years ago, I lost someone.
He died.
He went away.
He disappeared.
Loss changed the way I share love.

Don't hold your love away from those you care about,
or from those that love and care about you.

Whether you are withholding love because you are bruised, because you feel uncomfortable, or because you don't know how to restart, BE BRAVE and fight to hold heart space.

This world is an amazing, beautiful place, and yet often we treat each other cruelly and without intention. We lose sight of each other's human frailty.

When you hold your heart away, the messages stop, the requests to be a part of your heart cease, the phone stops ringing with hope on the other end that you will answer. The person who loves and cares about you may go away, may disappear.

So, love big, love intensely, love wide open and hold heart space.

Branches

Her arms reach toward the shining sun
Dropping an acorn now and again
Hoping one will germinate
Into a beautiful strong tree of its own.

She comes from a long line of oaks storing wisdom within
the rings of her trunk.
Her strength is like no other oak tree.
Her branches reach out further than any other.
They reach out to all she holds dear.
She comforts and loves all in her embrace.

She is the mother of all the oak trees that come after her.
She wraps each in a blanket of love as she sends them off into the world
Tall, short, twisted, or majestic,
Her acorns take root and grow as they may-
Each one unique from the other.
Some are strong and propagate other strong oaks to carry on her wisdom
Some develop disease and perish.
Some do not receive the sun's warmth delaying growth and losing
memory of the ancestors and their place in the line of oaks before them.

The last few years have cast shadow on the mother of all oak trees.
Her branches dry and brittle, fewer leaves greet each passing season
Her trunk may bend, but she is the symbol of strength, nobility and
knowledge that all of her acorns hope to grow into from underneath
her loving branches.

When we keep our hearts CLOSED, we become brittle and break easily. When we OPEN our hearts, we become soft and are able to BEND to all that life brings.

ACKNOWLEDGEMENTS

To my family and friends who have been the constant cheerleaders throughout this process. Thank you for believing in me. Your love and belief have helped make this possible.

To Kate Spencer, who first published my *Brave Enough To Love Me* affirmation in her book, *2018 Twelve Lessons Journal.*

To my editor, Crystal Roy, thank you for your vision and guidance throughout this process. Your understanding of my heart made these pieces come to life. I am forever grateful for your participation and friendship. Thank you for helping me share my voice and structure it in a way that it tells of the journey a heart can take at any given moment.

To my mother and father who understood my silence as a child and cultivated it into the voice that I hear within. They reminded me that feelings and words don't have to be spoken to be felt and heard. Their quiet, gentle guidance has always been ever-present.

Thank you to the universe for providing me with many muses. Thank you for allowing me to be aware enough of the significance of their presence.

To the many people who inspire me on a daily basis. I am amazed at your stories, your perseverance, your fearlessness, your fortitude, your strength, your vulnerability and your bravery. Keep shining your light, heart warriors.

ABOUT THE AUTHOR

Heidi Dellaire, BA, LMT, RAP, is an alternative health care practitioner, massage therapist, heart space coach and social entrepreneur. She is the founder and CEO of LoveWideOpen.com, a website for self-development centered around heart space healing and learning. Several of Heidi's poems have been published within articles at LoveWideOpen.com. Love Wide Open is a registered trademark. Heidi delivers a daily inspirational message to over 3 million souls on her Love Wide Open social media platforms and website. She is a lover of nature and finds her inspiration from the ocean or within the mountains. She lives in Maine, a place that will always be home to her heart.

Connect with author Heidi Dellaire at:

LoveWideOpen.com
HeidiDellaire.com
facebook.com/lovewideopen
facebook.com/heididellaireofficial
youtube.com/lovewideopen
instagram.com/lovewideopen
twitter.com/lovewideopen